This World needs to understand that some things 'that shouldn't be said out loud' are the most normal things to exist. If we continue hiding behind these things, change will never happen.

Selin Sara went on this road to see change among the ones, who sometimes forget that we become living through peace and kindness, with loyalty, love, trust, equality and humanity being her priority. She is a 21-year-old university student from Germany, who found her passion in writing, singing and painting.

Selin Sara

Awaken, Broken Soul

AUSTIN MACAULEY PUBLISHERS™

LONDON • CAMBRIDGE • NEW YORK • SHARJAH

A CIP catalogue record for this title is available from the British Library.

ISBN 9781398436343 (Paperback)
ISBN 9781398436350 (ePub e-book)

www.austinmacauley.com

First Published 2022
Austin Macauley Publishers Ltd
1 Canada Square
Canary Wharf
London
E14 5AA

„Mein Engel,
Wir sind so stolz auf dich, egal wie es ausgeht.
Bitte mach dir keine Sorgen, hinter jeder Nacht kommt die
Sonne auf.
Die schönsten Tage warten auf dich."

– Annem, Babam, Denizim

ACKNOWLEDGMENTS

You inspired me to end this book in strength and love
towards life.
While it was so hard sometimes to see light and hope
between misery.
You believed in me and encouraged me to never leave the
pen,
that made me breath again with each page written.
So, thank you, I love you more than anything.
This is for you, Mom and Dad,
my beloved brother,
Grandma
and SSSA,
my family.

Awaken, Broken Soul

Selin Sara

This is a story
About a princess
Who was seeking for good.
Who was seeking for a love
Coming from herself.
Who was seeking for a better life.

A princess
Whose tale
Worked with more than a shoe
Made of glass.

I will start right away. Throwing you into life. Showing you the face of a pessimist. Telling you a story about your own kind of Misery. When you tended to lose indication for yourself. Because you started living within the beginning it threw you in? I will start right away. Wanting you to read each line advisedly, to understand what I am actually trying to tell you. Between all this scorn please read in between the lines. And try to see the beauty and value I attempt to prove you.

I want to find you
In this dark chapter
That should be ended
And rewritten.
I want to find you,
My love.
You have been lost for too long.
Ready to be reborn in lives beauty
And happiness.

Unfetter me,
You who looks me so deeply in the eye.
Rescue me,
From this uncongenial confinement.
Safe us.

Take me out of this
Brokenness
I've been captured in
For too long.
Dig me out of this
Desperateness
I've been trapped in
For decades.

Usually
It's the tiniest things
That eventually becomes a crushing burden.
At the end,
When hundreds of trivialities
Follow on top of each other,
It's more
Than hard to
Keep a smiling face,
To think positive.

Fuck trivialities.
Because for me,
Those tiny things
Were massive.

So, let us start a journey to the past, to the day it started. The Day you decided to let go of your own two hands and make yourself be captive in a life that could only be lived in Black and White. The Day you forgot how to see in Color. Why did you forget to see the colors, my love?

When the rain is pouring down
The days don't seem to end

🖤

When suddenly night appears
The stars
And the Moon
Light up in small shadows of darkness
It seems like
There is no one there
To hold you tight
To dry your tears

When it's cold outside
And you are longing for warmth.
On a cloudy day
Imagining the Sun.

To the ones who know

There are some things
That can only be explained
Through experiences.
Thus these things
Will start making sense.

You can't hide who you really are
My Dad once said.
You can't hide the things you've experienced in life.
Experiences that define you.
Memories that suit you.
Explanations that built you.

I hate people
Who assume your life is perfect
And judge you for it
Though they ain't knowing nothing about it

- perks of being a good actor.

Dead of night
Captured me
In the past.
Memories
Ripped me
In thoughts.

Not knowing what life really is.
Not knowing the difference
Between Good and Bad,
Happiness and suffer.
- being a child

The princess was hiding
Underneath her bed
To overhear their fights.
A five year old girl
Already sick of hearing this brokenness
Every Day.

Now a 23 year old girl
Unable to believe in love.

I believe
That there is good in you
You
Who hurt
Betrayed
Lied to me.
And I do also believe
That there is bad in me.
Me
The one
Who believed in you all.
- yin yang

Initially
I let go of all the demons from my past
Though they seem to come back.
And I am so scared of it
Breaking me fully apart this time.

I was in third grade
When you told me
I was fat and ugly
When you observed my body
Full of disgust
When you left red paint
On my chin
And leg
That dripped down
So watery
With the ocean in my eyes
When you created fashion
By ripping
My favorite shirt apart
When you laughed
About my loyalty
Towards a friend
Who has never been
An actual friend
- bullies' wounds stay.

You formed the broken inside me.
You created the damage.
All starting when I was in my mothers womb.
You all made this good heart
Become a stranger to its owner.
You who beat a four year old's mother
In front of her eyes.
You as her brother.
You who treated us like misfits
In our own family.
You who made a pregnant woman
Feel insecure in her own skin.
I felt it too.
I was there.
You who deceived your own blood
Making your brother
Your Son
Live in famine and poverty.
You who let him drown in an addiction
To forget his sorrow.
Things that cannot be said out loud.
You who bullied and beat me up
For the 8 year old Girl I was.
Then laughing about it another 6 years later.
You
You
You
You formed this.
You created this.

You
My beloved uncle
Who then
Called me
Mentally disturbed.
Cause you couldn't handle
Your own sickness.
You couldn't handle
Your own fucked up life
And carved up family.

You
My beloved uncle
Who then
Made an 11 year old Girl
Question those words
The older she got.

Did I even know what mental health was?

I didn't.

                                      But he wanted me to.

He wanted me to believe

                  That I was more screwed up than his daughter.

That my Mom was more vulnerable,

                              Than him.

And what if I am?
Is that a crime then?

You can be forced to live a love-hate relationship with people, who do not even deserve your hate. That may sound harsh, but we live in a world where equity is a loanword for almost everyone. Even for people you are related with. It nearly feels like you are at war, a war where everyone has to be better than anyone. Where emotions are controlled by jealousy and prejudice. Where people hold other people for granted, cause they are content with their lives. That's a world we live in. And that's usually what families are made of. Who has the biggest car. Who owns the best house. Who has the best children. Whose kid is the smartest. Who is mostly fucked up. I know that I am. And my Aunt is, my Uncle, all my cousins. All of us, in our own way.

Sometimes Family is only an expression
Used for a bunch of people,
Who may share the same bloodline,
But make you understand,
That even water can be thicker.

You all created this.
You formed this.

Until it sank in.
And made me
Who I Am Now.

When you show your weakness
People tend to break you.

I am not telling you this to arouse pity for anybody who struggles with family issues of any kind. For the one who struggles with bullies and the consequences it brings. I am telling you this to understand that there needs to be a change, starting with yourself. Talking to the one who bullies and the one who got bullied. Talking to the one who treats their own family irrationally and non-existent. The one who acts primitive and selfish. The one who still holds on to something that should long be gone. I am not telling you this to judge, because we all know that nobodies life is perfect. Yours isn't, mine isn't, theirs isn't. I am telling you this to see the light between the black and white. Because everything leaves a good and bad impact, you only have to place the higher weight on the valuable one.

You hated me for nothing.
So,
For a Short time
Hurting myself seemed like a result.

Till I hated myself
More than the people who brought me to that point.
I hated myself
And that broke me.

To my Broken Soul

I'm sorry for never telling you
That you weren't the problem.
That I was.
That I hated the person I was.
- I am so sorry.

Ben niye böyleyim diye diye
Kendimden nefret etmeyi öğrendim.

Kendimi sevmekten
Daha çok kin ile beslendim.

It hurts to be betrayed
By people
You thought would never hurt you.
The betrayal of love,
Of trust.
- Betrayal sucks

I'm orbited by wrong people.

So I drowned in a

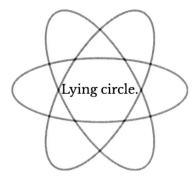

Lying circle.

Empty words
Followed by
Emotional eyes.

Don't lie to yourself.

You still love
Don't you?
The same way I did.

Still loving the ones
Who call themselves
Friends.
The ones
Who call themselves
Family.

- we still love

I was hoping
My wounds would heal.

And they did.

Not every wound disappears
Without leaving its mark.

- the formation of scars

What's the use of a healing wound anyway,
If a whole piece of painful memories are left.

I'm sick.

I'm sick of counting my scars.

Sick in my fucking head.

As a kid
Everything seemed easier
Even though life was difficult sometimes
I was still living in a world
Full of magic and fantasy

- the proof that Fairy Godmother exists

You know what the worst type of feeling is?
Waking up every morning
Hating another day to live.
Falling asleep every night
Tired of another day passed.
You know what the worst type of feeling is?
Not feeling happy
While pretending.
Not feeling alive
While living.

You are ugly.
You are stupid.
You are nothing but useless.
You will never be loved.
You deserve to be alone.
You won't achieve anything in life.

- things I've told myself

Is it normal to hate your birthday?
Reminds me of a life I never wanted to live.
And a World I never wanted to be part of.
Sad isn't it?

All this time
I felt like I wasn't enough.
Seeing nothing but
Hate,
Disgust,
Pain.
- struggles of self-love

I didn't feel like I was part of them.
I never did.
Not cause they didn't love me.
They did everything they could
To make me happy.
But sometimes it just doesn't work that way.

> They did all of these things,
> Even more,
> Never wanted anything back.
> Accepted all my flaws.

And I felt like
They were too good for someone like me.
Somebody sick of life
And herself.

When am I gonna be enough.

When am I gonna be good enough.

I've been crying all night
To soften my soul
To free my heart.
But the more I cried
The more I ended up

In a black hole.

I tried to love myself,
I really did.
But every time I looked in the mirror
I hated what I see
I hated every inch that defined me.

I thought it's impossible
For someone to love me.
I didn't understand
That the only love
I needed
Was the one from myself.
But that love didn't exist anyway.

Sometimes the love
Of your parents
Just doesn't seem enough.

And I'm so sorry to feel this way...

I understood that it is normal to question yourself sometimes, to have doubts and feel like everything is losing control. I understood that it is normal to not feel okay, to be needy, to not feel like leaving bed and crying. Not even knowing what you are crying about. I understood that it is normal to not feel yourself at times. Feeling beautiful and strong. Weakness isn't a lower self-esteem, a bad mood, having trust issues and flaws, falling in love with the wrong person, being scared or having insecurities. That doesn't make you weak, it makes you human. I understood that life has its ups and downs, since the ups are more valuable they can and always will overcome the downs.

What does love even mean?

According to Google it's the
attachment to a particular human being based on a strong
physical, mental, emotional attraction,
combined with a desire for
togetherness, surrender or similar.
- Is that love?

If that's the definition of love,
Why can't I ,
Me,
Myself
Be the particular human being.
- love me.

why?

To her passenger

The twenties are the worst.
You just ended puberty
And then this time starts
Where you don't really know
What life's gonna bring you next.

Sorry about my negativity,
But life didn't ask for permission either,
When it past me its.

Can you hear me
When hope
Starts fading away
And I need a hand
To pull me up again
From this depth?

Because hope is the only thing
That somehow keeps you alive.
While everything else seems to drown.

Or, Hope itself can drown you in an abyss of sickness

I'm exhausted
Of being strong
All the time
While it feels like
Even my own feet
Can't carry me anymore.

I'm so tired
Of waiting
I'm so tired
Of fighting

Today I let myself go,
For the first time in my life.
I abated myself into a glass of oblivion
And i feel no regret.
- *touchdown*

Words expressing hurt
Emotions written through a pen
Held by dithering hands
Blue ink seen through
Glassy eyes
Pages filled with years of
Adventures
Sufferings
Love
life.

It feels like I can't breathe.
I need to leave
To find oxygen
Filling up my body.

Bazen kuslar gibi uçmak istiyorum.
Uzaklara.

Have you
ever thought about
taking some random flight to
abandon the despair that
follows you?

Every day the same old people
Every day the same old town
Every day the same

The passenger was living within her. Telling her to breathe in and out, while looking out the window. While writing her final exams. While being at the hospital and waiting for the results. While sitting inside the plane. While laying in the backyard, watching bees make love to their flowers. While sipping on her coffee. While talking to her Husband. While fighting. While laughing. While crying. While screaming. The passenger was living within her. At midnight, at sunrise, at Noon. Living within her thoughts and feelings. Making her feel sensitive, loved, sad, scared, unpredictable, sentimental, egoistic, secure. Living within her desires. That kept her body warm and intensive. That kept her from going down while she wanted to let go of everything. The passenger was living within her. Living within her own four walls. Talking to her like Lucifer and Lilith. Like Hades seeking for his powers. Like Poseidon forming his hurricanes. Like Pan Gu creating life. Like Peter never growing old. Talking to her like an Angel brought to find peace. The passenger was living within her. And made her live within her own kind of milky way. Being her own asteroids, planets, stars. Being her own moon and sun and earth. The passenger was living within her and made her living.

Waking up at 3 AM.
Filled with aspirations
To start something new
To see
To experience
To meet
Something
Someone new
- craving

At times I feel like
I'm stuck,
Stuck in a tiny little capsule.
Feeling like a goldfish
In an aquarium.
- watching life pass by

Sometimes I wish Space would take me
Far away From here

I've always wondered
How it'd be like
Living on the moon
- could I be myself there?

Days pass
And i fall
Deeper
into an
Abyss.

Days where happiness seems miles away.

I don't know what to feel,
My body is empty
My heart overwhelmed
My emotions
Too much to take
My life
A blurry Canvas.

Telling the moon my problems
To see everything more clearly.
Trying to catch a piece of sun
To lighten the darkness.

❄ I'm like snow water
Ready to melt
Bringing spring's beauty
Back to life
In summers bright
Transforming into
Colorful canvas of autumn
Letting winters cold
Be born
All over again.

I've always wondered where *happy* would be
                                    It's where your soul feels the safest
Where your mind feels the smoothest
                          And your heartbeat feels the most uniform

Her Passenger has never been a stranger.
She couldn't see
Could not understand
Could not feel
That the passenger has always been
Herself.
A warm
And beautiful feeling
That made her
Just human.

The deepest darkness
Drowned me in pieces of memories
And thoughts.
Upon the sky,
Only parts of light stars.
My mind,
With you.
Sleep,
Miles away.
- Midnight

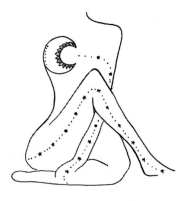

To my first Love

He was a complicated
Hard and
Broken man.
But I didn't care,
The only thing I knew
Was that I could love him.
But my love was too much for him to take.

I am sitting here
Looking at pages
Ready to be filled
With you.

You
Who knows my whole heart
Who enchanted my Soul
You
Whom I so deeply love

I did not know you could fall in love that fast.
Apparently love doesn't know any time.

Once it hits you, It doesn't leave.

Ömrümün sonuna kadar seni devam seveceğim. Hayatımı senin kokunla, dudaklarının tadıyla, saçlarının dökümüyle, kendi nefesim gibi, içime sindireceğim. Hayat çok garip, boşlukta hissettiğin bir an, bir sahnede herşey gibi içine doğar. Mutluluk, Huzur, Aşk birden herseyin olmaya başlar. Tıpkı senin gibi. Sen benim Mutluluğum, Huzurum, Sevgim, Aşkım, Gülbahçemdeki ~okum, Yatak Odamın Işığı, Kalbimin Şiiri oldun. ilk defa kelebeklerin gerçek olduğunu anladım. Her Ev, Sokak, Rüzgar, Kelime bir Hatıra olmaya başladı. Yüzümdeki bitmeyen bir gülümseme gibi, sen yokken o hatıralar ile yaşadım, varken gülümseyişleri o Hatıralarla doldurdum. Sensiz olan bir Hayat, Dünya yok oldu. Kapıldım sana., senki çaldın kalbime giden killedin anahtarını. Ey Aşk, nereye sakladın gözlerimin önünde olan bu gerçeğini.

I will continue loving you until the end of my life. I will fill my life with your scent, the taste of your lips, the falling of your hair, like my own breath. Life is so strange, a moment when you feel trapped in emptiness can change in a second to being everything. Happiness, peace, Love suddenly becomes all you have. Just like you. You have become my Happiness, My Peace, My Love, my scent in my Garden full of Red Roses, the Light of my Bedroom, the Poem of my Heart. For the first time, I realized that the butterflies do really exist. Every House, Street, Wind, Word has become an important Memory. Like an endless smile on my face, I lived with those memories while we were not together, and when you were there I filled these smiles with every possible Memory. A Life, World without You did not exist anymore. I fell for you, while you tended to steel the key to my heart. O Love, how did you hide this fact in front of my love-filled eyes.

How can everything
Be one person?
How can everything
Cover-up one soul?

When I was on vacation
You told me
That I finally was at my happy place
I said yes
Whispering
The only happy place for me
Is next to you.

Hello love,
On this cloudy
Rainy day.
Hello,
To your smiling face.

Your lips
Touching mine
Our bodies
Form one
Your heart
My home
Your hug
A feeling of
Certainty.
Our skins connecting
An obligation.

Sitting on your lap
Sucking every inch of your body.
Kissing you
Feeling you
Loving you.

I want to inhale you
Till my lungs are filled
I want to peck you
Till my mind feels high
I want to pull you deeper
Till my body is incapable
Shaking through every sensitivity.
- yes, sex is natural

I did not know
The smell of a person
So close to your heart
Can be like
Medicine
For your soul.
- Tom Ford

I fell in love with your music taste.
Words
Melodies
That felt like
I was losing you
Every time I listen to them.
- 24/7

You became my life's metaphor.
A story,
That didn't need any hyperbole
To describe our love.

But
Love is relative.

And we are,
We are like a puzzle
With missing pieces.
Never fully one picture.

Nevertheless
Capricorns
Do not fall for
Capricorns.

- with you astrology started

She was a girl
Supposed to walk down the streets
All by herself.
She was a girl
Never supposed to
Meet you.

According to chemistry
Attractions between
Atoms and molecules
Create a bond
That shares
Strength and
interactions.
However
Using the wrong bond
Makes the attraction
collapse.
Their chemistry never
Interacts.
Some chemicals
Are just not
Made for each other
To connect.
- Us.

My Mom always said,
That you won't forget your first love.
I never understood what she meant.

                                        But when I lost him...

Well,
Then I knew.

(your first love's memories and pain will never fully decay, I guess.)

The moment I couldn't call you mine
Couldn't call you a friend
Couldn't call you part of my life.
The moment you became a stranger,
Loneliness filled my body
And loss became my lifestyle.

Don't take my heart with you
When you leave.

Just take the part that belongs to you
And then
Go.

My heart shattered
Into millions of pieces
The moment I realized
You belong to another woman.
Yet, I still waited.
- soulmates

I didn't know how it feels like
To fall in love
So when I met you
I was overwhelmed
With emotions
That made me feel
So fucking good
And scared
All at once.
- Love

Am I falling in love too fast?
Am I a slut for letting him in?
Is he using me?
Is he feeling the same way, I do?
Am I overwhelming him?
Am I too sticky?
Is he still interested?
Did I mess up?
Is he a Fuck-boy?
Why isn't he texting?
Can I trust him?
Is he hating me?
Am I not his type?
Is he still gonna like me,
Once he knows me?
Why can't I stop thinking about him?
- the beginning

You know it doesn't shock me
That we didn't work out.
I come from a family
Whose relationships have always been
Messed up.

Over the years
A lot of people hurt and left me.
Friends
Family.
Over time
It felt like,
I was a girl
Impossible to love.

I became skeptical
That I
Instead of loving and being happy
Built a Wall
Closing every possible way
Into my Heart.

So when he left
Like the other ones.
I hated myself more than him.

Another person you couldn't keep in your life.

I'm waiting for you, my love.
Though you're long gone.
I'm still waiting,
Always waiting for you.

Where are you
When I awaken
At midnight.

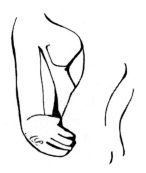

Where are you
When I turn to my left,
Seeing emptiness.

I fall asleep every night with my arms around
the Sweater you gave me when I was freezing
cold. It keeps me warm, yes. But it also makes
me feel secure. It makes me feel like you are
right next to me and your smell... God, the
smell of this piece of fabric... so real, so
soothing. I fall asleep every night with my
arms around the Sweater you gave me.
Because it is the only thing I have left from
you. So I fall asleep with my arms around the
Sweater you gave me, only imagining the
smell coming from your neck.

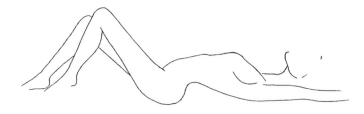

I miss you
And god
Missing you
Is worse than anything else.

Another
Day
Month
Year passed
With only your memory
Being my sanctuary.
Time is relative.
But with you in my head
It seems eternal.

I would prefer
Seeing you every day
With this pain
Instead of
Imagining your
Appearance.

I tried to escape you
Your smile
Your laugh
Your eyes
Your lips
Your warmth
Your hug
I tried to escape everything
That made me think about you.
But the more I tried
The more I ended up in a dead end.
- process of forgetting him.

First Day
They text, rather holding back but still committed.

First week
They make you understand, that they are interested and start texting more and more.

First Month
They give you the Maximum amount of attention.
Attention you do not want neither care about.
Till you get you used to their kindness and gentlemanlike behavior.

Till you get used to them.

Loving the person they present you.
Somebody, who became someone really important, in such a short time.
You decide, you want to trust them, to start opening up.
You decide you want them to know the real you, who was so scared of showing her true self.

And suddenly...

They stop.

Half a year later
You look back at your old text messages.
Wondering if that was still the same person.
Somebody who acted like he wanted to be part of your life so urgently...
Now, someone who can't even ask you,
how you are doing.

I was too stubborn to call,
But why were you?
I was too hurt to call,
But why were you?
I was too proud to call,
But why were you?

I was suffering for months,
Trying to live without you again,
But were you?

I'm
waiting
for
a
call
That's
never
gonna
come.

And
the
worst
part
is,

I still have hope.

You think I didn't care
But ask the people around me
Witnessing my pain
Each day,
After us ended.
- before I decided to call you

There it is,

This so familiar voice.

Like music in my ears.

Saving my soul

For the first time

In months.

I knew you never cared

About me.

But hearing you,

One last time,

Brought peace

Into my aching heart.

One last time
I want to look
Into your
Blurry grey eyes

One last time
I want to feel
The warmth of
Your hug

One last time
I want to smell
The bitter-sweet
Fragrance
Of your skin

One last time
I want to be
The one
That enlightens
Your day

One last time
I want to create
A memory
In your mind.
A beautiful memory

One last time
I want to be
yours.
And I want you
To be mine.

Please do something
Yell at me
Hurt me.
Show me all your negative sides.
Do something
So that I can hate you.
Cause right now
I suffer from our beautiful memories.
I blame myself for losing you.
And that fucking hurts.

L
I
V
I
N
G

In a bottle
of
Painful and
Beautiful
Memories.

I'm thinking about a time before you.

Never really delighted,

But never this deep in hopelessness.

They say if somebody really loves you
This person will fight for not losing you.
No matter what happened.

And maybe they are right.

But what if I love this person way too much,
To oversee him not fighting.

Waking
up every
morning To catch
a piece of
sun That
enlightens Midnight
memories.

Am I a bad person
The princess asked.
No, she said.
You only love
Too deeply.

Cause love
Knows no criteria.
You simply
Love.

Toxic

Your attention
Seemed like love
I just now realize
It was the most toxic
Feeling I ever felt.
- your love was nothing but toxic

You called me a child
Till the 2 year old inside me
Died
And lost her happiness.

Can't you see?
I started to love you
More than myself.
I started to care
About you more
Than
Myself.
Hate arouse
Towards
Myself.
Can't you see?
That broke me.

Life was easier
When you wasn't
Part of my memory
Part of my heart
Part of my thoughts
Part of my everything

It's crazy
How one person
Can shatter
Your rebuilt
Self-courage

It's crazy
How one person
Can shatter
Things you once lost
And then found again

And then lost again.

You can't admit it to yourself.
But you know,
You lost him
You know,
He doesn't love you
You know,
He doesn't want you

- confirmations you can't stand to hear

But you need to hear them.
You need to listen now.

You promised
But
I just now
Realized
that your promises
Meant nothing.
- your promises have never been something to hold on to

It took you a month
To make me fall for you.
It took me years
To make me forget you.

However

It took you seconds
To dowse me.

It took you picoseconds
To make me drown
In a love
That was never supposed to be mine.

And you knew.

Sometimes I wish I would have never known you.

But it is good that I did,
Now I know what to avoid
The next time.

You knew
You were my first
In everything
And you hated me
For being scared of love
For being a virgin
In any possible way.
- when they say they want a *well-behaved* girl, they hate you even more
    for not having any *experience*

Blaming myself for everything
That happened
However
I wonder if you were ever
Seeking for the mistakes
In yourself.

yes,
i would have done a lot of things differently
but i am not the one to blame for us falling apart.

How could I possibly be talking about mistakes,
When he wasn't even man enough to call back?
How could I be so foolish,
Seeing all the good inside you
While you tended to turn me against myself.
I insisted Me
Because of you.

if
love really
means to always
blame yourself for the
bad things happening then
I don't wanna
fall for
it

You didn't
You don't
Even know
How much
Your words
Hurt me.

Based on
the way
you talk
to me,
Your eyes
tell a whole
other story.

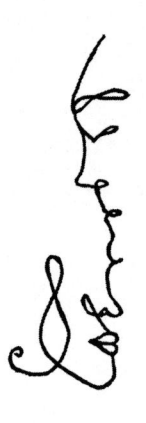

My brittleness
Became your
Strength.

My reclusion
Became your
Power.

My affinity
Became your
Oblivion.

My grief
Became your
Past.

To be honest
I feel so
Worthless
Dumb
Gratuitous
While talking to you,
Thinking about you.

My feelings for you
Make me feel nugatory
towards myself.

My cousin once told me:
Never date a man who loves himself more than you.
Because if he does, you will never be his priority.
Like he is yours.

You need to understand that loving and wanting someone is not the same as needing someone. Do not confound those two things. You need Air to breathe, you need Water to survive, you need Sunlight to see life, you need Night to fall asleep, you need Nature to be alive. Needing somebody is something different. You do not need him. You are unbounded and the best, yes, even without him.

so,
I realized
seeing you
one last time
wasn't a good bye.
it was
the beginning
of a
Valuable
and Better
life

I cried
And cried
And cried
Till one day
I realized
Why cry over somebody
Who didn't want to stay
At the first place.
- understand who is worth your tears

My
love for you
Was eternal But I
am talking in
past tense,

Even eternity can suspend.

Do not value someone who gave everything at the beginning and once they knew you fell for them, left you incomplete. Value someone who looks at you, the same way, they did from when you first met. Who admires you even more, day by day, especially after knowing all your flaws. Value someone who doesn't see you as a trophy he can win at the end of a race. Once he got you, you will end up next to all the old metal sheets. Somebody who accepts your past and won't judge you for it. Somebody who listens, to your insecurities, secrets, dreams, memories. Value someone who appreciates your friendship and commitment. Value someone who respects you for the woman you are. Who sees the beauty inside and out. Somebody who won't make you feel insecure in your own body. Somebody who lets you know that you are strong and stunning, when you tend to forget. Value someone who loves every bit about you. Even the tiniest things. Somebody who loves how you wake up in the morning. How you moan about unnecessary things. How red you get when they compliment you. How you drink your coffee. How you laugh at your favorite sitcom. How excited you get when you talk about your Day. How you close your eyes, sitting on the gras, the sun shining bright onto your beautiful face. How much you care about people. How you talk to your cat. How worried you get, when you miss a call by somebody you love. How you pet your plants. How upset you get, when they forgot the ketchup to your fries at the DriveThrough. How much you eat when you are on your period. How needy you are at times. Maybe all the time. Value someone who won't make you lose yourself. Somebody who is going to be there, on your good as well as bad days. Value them. Not the ones who fuck up your soul.

There will be a better one.
Who will treat you admirably and preciously.
Like you deserve.
Do not search for that person,
Let time handle it.
And through that time,
Even after,
Treat You
The right way as well.

To our society

I started to cover myself.

Covering myself to hide the parts

That defined me.

But the Question was:

For What?

- struggles of being yourself

1 2 5 0

1250 calories a day it said.
Counting every bite.
Counting every bit of food.
That would make it
Be acceptable for him.
For them.
For me.?!
- counting calories to sharpen perfection

I watched my body grow
Until the stripes started to the show themselves.
Until I saw nothing
But a creature
That looked like she wasn't enough
For *society*.
Until I started to try
To be *perfect*
But failed.

- Does perfection even exist?

Don't show too much, they said.
Don't look at him, they said.
Don't do eye contact, they said.
Don't let him know, they said.
Don't make him understand, they said.
Don't talk too much, they said.
Don't do parties, they said.
Don't drink, they said.
Keep your reputation, they said.

- what if I just fuck what they've said

The only thing I wanted
Was to talk to somebody
About what I wanted to experience
And what I had experienced
Without being told
That it is wrong to feel that way.
- opening up without being judged

Slut.Whore.Bitch.Hoe.

Does a good reputation
save me

from these words?

Yes,
I am a woman.
But my breasts and hips
Aren't the only things that define me.

To the ones
Who are not willing to accept it.
Feminism does exist.
Especially in a men-ruled world.

Plus.
The World needs women.
Without women
Men would lose their minds.

I am not a female creature.
I am a goddamn human,
Like you are.
Sorry,
That I just don't own a Dick.

172

'Believe it or not
Woman can be friends
With people with dicks
And not
Hop on them.'
- Ariana Grande

Being yourself
By either walking around half naked
Or dressed like a nun
By drinking, smoking and partying all night
Or sitting at home and doing nothing
By being totally different than others
Still being part of a movement
By either believing in my religion with all my heart
Or not believing in anything
By having mental health issues
And by being strong
By being male,
female,
diverse,
straight,
gay,
tall,
small,
big,
thick,
thin,
Blond,
Brown,
Red,
White,
Black,
Orange,
Purple,
Fucking Pink

I have depressions.

That doesn't make me
Crazy
Neither devastated.

I'm hurt.

And that shattered me.

People love to talk about the way you dress, the way you talk, how many friends you have, especially male ones. People love to talk about your mental health, your family problems, your income and how much money you have on your bank account. People love to talk about your sex life, your relationships, your insecurities, how much you weight, how perfect your life is. What people do not like to talk about is the truth. About their own mental health, the world, global warming, relationships, insecurities, flaws, income and their perfect life. People like to judge, because what you see on the outside always creates the perfect image. But the actual truth will always be a secret. So people need to stop talking. And start wondering about their own truths.

Society
Makes us live a life we never wanted to live.
Society
Makes us become somebody we never wanted to be.

I think we have to get over these barriers
That hold us back.
We have to start
To change our minds
To change the norms of society.
Once we get over these borders,
peace will seem closer than ever.

195 countries
6500 languages
7 770 000 000 people
1 race

There is only one race
And we are all part of it.
        - human

Redundant

And

Cruel

Expression

I'm *Muslim*

But I'm also
Christian
Jewish
Buddhist
Hindu
Atheist

I'm *Turkish*

But I'm also
German
French
Spanish
Polynesian
Russian
Italian
Nigerian
Japanese
Costa Rican
- etc.

Our personalities,
Beliefs,
Orientations,
The way we look on the outside,
May be different from each other.
Nevertheless,
Looking more closely
On the inside
We are all the same.

We are attendees in this world,

We should act like ones.

You do not have to be Vegan or Vegetarian to see how we treat the living
on our earth.
How we stop life for jewelry that fits so perfectly on our neck.
How we cease existence for a finesse on our skin.
How we destroy something
That deserves life as much as we do.
No, not something.
Somebody.
- My Cat is a She

How selfish can human nature be?
Destroying a world made for us to live in.
Building obstacles among the ones
We are formed to be with
The ones like you
Me
Them
Us.

How selfish can human nature be?
Actually ready to fill our earth
With millions of omissions
Through a gratuitous war,
We wanted to be part of ?
- learn from history

I want to tell you the Story of a Turkish saying my Grandma once told me about. Once upon a time, in a small village called Akşehir, there was living a rich landlord whose reputation was all known in town. How could a poor townsman know how classy and honorable it is to be invited to one of his Dinner Parties? When the landlord invited Nasrettin, a normal Man with a normal life to one of his Organizations, he attended, as usual, without any specialties in his daily outfit. As soon as he entered the hall, there were people dressed in scarlet, scaly clothes. None of them paid any attention to the man who looked like a typical citizen, missing any golden accessories and any sign of money. Thereupon Nasrettin made his way home quickly, pulled his coat of embroidered fur over his chest and went back to the dinner party. The ones who couldn't even look at him and greet him before where now bowing down to his knees. The equivalent of the air had now become the king of the evening, all kinds of attention being devoted to the once poor Nasrettin. When they were all seated at the dining table Nasrettin, of course at the head of the table, was served the best piece of lamb and everyone was just waiting for him to start eating. However, Nasrettin was shocked at how selfish and wrong people had behaved. He just looked at them all and waved at the table with the sleeve of his fur, saying: "Eat my fur, eat my fur!"

It's sad
How we are programmed
To live a life
That's about money
Success
School
Work
Perfection

                                        Besides

                    Peace
                    Love
                    And
                  Cohesion.

Why did you bring me to a World, where
Hate,
Racism,
Sexism,
War,
Discrimination,
Harm
exist.
Why did you let me experience a World, where
Happiness isn't the only thing
You get to see.
- Questions we ask our parents

I wish I could be someone
With a heart full of hate
Someone
Just like them
Wishing everyone the worst
Being jealous from the deepest point of my soul
I wish I could be the bad one
For once

**But I ain't
And I never will.**

However
In a world
Full of
Greed
Jealousy
Bigotry
Prejudice
Violence
Betrayal

A world like this

Where good people barely exist

Needs us.

I do not get
What's so hard for people to understand.
We do not have to look for a segregation
By talking about Borders
Countries
Companies
Bank Accounts
Politics
Beliefs.
We have to look for a solidarity
That brings us all together.
Nevertheless,
At the end
All of us
End up
In the same place.
Earth.

To Us

All the things written in here
Short but meaningful sentences
Built a wall inside the princess,
A wall of fear.
The princess was so scared of getting hurt,
So she acted like
Whoever wants to get into her life,
Will soon be ready to leave.
To avoid that
She behaved prudently.
She repelled anything
That might make her vigorous again.

All the things written in here
Made the princess feel like
She wasn't worth
Being loved
And respected
Being a woman
Being strong
And feeling beautiful
Being human
And living.
Living life the way she wanted to.

All the things written in here
Made the princess feel sick
Sick of everything
Every closed door that wouldn't let her
Be the Girl she wanted to be.

The princess had everything
But everything sometimes
Just doesn't feel enough.

Yes, the princess had everything.

But she has never really been happy
And happiness means more than anything.
Because through happiness
Follows peace and love

With the world

And most importantly

With <u>yourself</u>.

Can you feel it?

It feels so cold in here.
This body that got hurt several times,
And froze into a glacier of
Despair.

Can you sense it too?

I found myself dreaming
For a life that was worth more
Than this one.
I found myself dreaming
For a life that was better living in
Than this one.
- in silver and gold

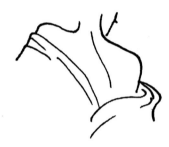

I feel neglected
By my missing contentment.

Where are you
When there is nothing
I can hold onto
Anymore.

5895588
I miss you
You who saw life's beauty once
I miss you
You who was fearlessly going through
Obstacles and borders
I miss you
You who
Was loving herself

I was looking for you.

I wanted to find you.

So, I did.

Shattering the wall that kept me from you.

Till the *princess*
Became the *QUEEN*

There she was,
Looking me so deeply in the eye.

You
Stranger
Take my hand
And I'll show you how to live again.

3112
Ending
To start new.

Now.

Awaken
Broken soul.

Awaken from this cage
You have been trapped in for too long.

I want you to understand, that you are worth being loved and fighting for. That you are worth living every possible happiness on this World, that you are worth being valued. I want you to understand, that you have to stop expecting others to believe in you. Start doing it yourself. I want you to understand, that you are perfect and beautiful in your own way. I want you to understand, that you are so goddamn precious. And that you don't have to let others treat you, like you are nothing. That you can let go of these toxic people. And toxic feelings. Because you are stronger than you think. I know that. You are free and full of self-esteem. Deep down you know it too. I want you to open your eyes and awaken from these dark thoughts that hold you back. Start seeing your own value, your actual flawlessness, your real confidence, your existent reflection inside that hiding mirror. Through that, peace, fulfillment and self-awareness will follow.

Sometimes you have to cross the street
To start a new path.

I'm leaving,
To build my own fucking Queendom.

You aren't able to control me anymore.
I'm a Queen
And every Queen
Follows her own rules.

The more I try to be perfect
The more I suck in it.
And it's okay not to be
Because perfection doesn't exist.
- the approval

On that Day
I looked in the mirror
And I decided
To accept my flaws.
I decided to love this person
Who formed her own kind of perfection.

On that Day
I started a new
A stronger Me.
I found myself.

On that Day
I was reborn in self-assurance.

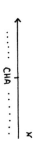

Healing is a long process
That makes you grow
Each time
Into the person
You are today.
Continuously.

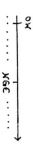

Self-love defines the kind, where you honor your quirks, look upon your good sides. and start accepting some repercussions in life. That's when you build up a desire of respect towards Yourself.

Yes, I own these scars
You all created.
And I am so proud of them.
If you were the ones to own them
You couldn't even handle their pain,
You couldn't even wear them with dignity.
Saying
'That's me
Stronger
And
More beautiful
Than ever before,
Cause you couldn't
And
Will never be able
To let me down.'

I had depressions
Because you wanted to see me fall apart
But I ain't giving you that power anymore.

I am not a toy you can buy at a store and throw away once it rusted, got damaged, lost its beauty – according to you. I have a heart, a soul, so I do not understand how somebody can be this cruel and acardiac. Sometimes I wonder if you were the ones who are exanimate, maybe a myth?

One thing I hated were lies.
No.
One thing I hate are lies.
And it feels like everyone is just doing
What I hate.
They are lying to me.

People make mistakes
Horrible
Terrible
Miserable ones.

I don't get
Why some people
Like to
Fuck
With other people's
lives.

A alguien
Que no es feliz
Le gusta hacer
La vida
Miserable
Para los demás.

Someone
Who ain't happy
Likes to make
Life
Miserable
For others.

But I'm done
Done being used
By the ones
Who aren't worth
My love and kindness.
- the beginning of acceptance

I'm done making myself a fool.
I won't force you to stay in my life.
If you wanna leave,
There's the door.
Literally f off.

If someone isn't giving you the same respect
They expect from you.
Then you are not indebted to show them any.

Though I ain't somebody
Who wishes anyone
Anything bad.
I hope that karma
Hits the people
That hurt me
Hard.
- 'cus karma is a bitch

If you won't accept
Respect
Understand
The way I fill in the blanks of my own story.
Then, leave me the fuck alone
And goddamn live your own darned life
That is according to you more ideal than mine.

- filling her Empire

You know,
It doesn't matter how good of a person you are.
If somebody is hurting you
Giving shit about you
Hating you
Deceiving you
Over and over again,
Then please let go.
Cause the more you let on
The more you will hurt yourself
And make them feel good
About
You giving a damn fuck
- sacred and empowered decisions

Watching the world from a different perspective.

You have to look for the right people
And leave the wrong ones
To find fulfillment.

Watching life from a different perspective.

Sometimes
It's good to let go.
It's the <u>best</u>.

From now on
I will choose me.
Cause I am the one
Who will hold me tight,
When I seem to fall.

I cried my way through bleak

Freezing in our last season.

Till a warm flare effaced my skin

Gelidity dissolved in free particles of lifegiving.

Desolation finally started fading away.

My existence a recommencement

In flowering elegance.

Cause I was more.
I was more than what they saw in me.
And how they treated me.
I was Me.
And that was more than okay.

Living in this fucked up world
By being human
By being me
Just *me*.

Sometimes being all by yourself,
Finding the balance between your
Mind,
Heart and
Soul,
Is the best kind of therapy.
- Redemption

Take some time to yourself,
Give yourself the same kind of love
You would have given
That *boy*
Who seemed like your only love.

Take some time to yourself,
Give yourself the same kind of attention
You would have given
Those liars and betrayers
Who seemed like friends
And family.

Take some time to yourself,
Give yourself the eternal adoration
You deserve.

Close this Chapter,
My love.
Open new doors
Among Zones
That start
And cease again.
Find yourself
My love,
Between these shores
Like a book flown
In Entity.

Scream Honey,
Run through this captivity
With open arms,
Breaking every bond
That seems like a fence
Towards elation.

Scream Honey,
Lighten your Soul,
Outline your brawn,
Let your voice be heard.

Life is full of ups and downs Honey
You need to find the balance between them.

Right now
It may doesn't seem that way.
Still,
It will get better.
You will be happy again.
You are capable of anything you want.
It only takes time
And strength.

One Day,
You will look back
And understand
That everything,
Even the bad things,
Happened for a reason.
Even though
You sometimes
Give a damn
About the reasons.

Never forget that you are loved

Never forget that you aren't alone

Never forget that you are beautiful

Never forget that you are strong

Never forget that you are free

Never forget that you are amazing

Never forget that you are special

Never forget that you are good

Never forget that it is okay.

I look at you

And the only thing I see

Is a beautiful

Strong

And precious woman.

Wow.

<u>Normal things</u>

Acting wrong.
Making Mistakes.
Talking shit.
Wanting to scream, cry, laugh, love
Feeling hate.
Feeling fortunate.
Mood changes.
Every second
Minute
Hour
Day.
Days where you have a couple more bites.
Days with the impurest skin ever.
Days where things won't go the way you want 'em to
At work
School
Home
Life.
Days where life just doesn't go the right way.

Things that need to be set clear

You don't need a Man in life
To rise
And boast like a thunder.

You don't have to play
By society's rules
To form your own kind of perfection.

Tell your kids
That bullying
Is never an option.

You do not have to
Hold on to toxic people
And toxic feelings.

Tell Men
To respect women
And stop raping.

Enjoy and appreciate
The little things.

You don't have to pretend
To be somebody else.
Just be fucking you.

Sometimes putting your pride
And stubbornness aside
Is the best thing you can do

You are more than enough.

Start working together
Not against each other.

It's okay
To not feel okay.

And most importantly
Do
Not
Overthink
Everything.
It will drive you crazy.

Is it a *bad thing*
To open up about your feelings
To admit that you're hurt
To say that you made a mistake
Is it a *bad thing*
To be who you want to be
And who you simply are
To want to live
Without the norms and rules
Society wants you to accept
Is it a *bad thing*
To be Muslim,
Christian,
Jewish,
Atheist,
Buddhist,
Hindu
and any religion existing
To believe
To be different
As an individual
To follow your own path
Is it a *bad thing*
To just be humankind?
- rhetorical questions you know the answer to

Αγάπη	Human
kärlek	Mensch
Milovat	İnsan
szeretet	menneskelige
Amor	Mens
meilė	njeriu
kærlighed	رجل
kærlighet	Մարդու
влюблённость	ljudski
liefde	човека
elska	ang tawo
ljubav	人类
amore	čovjeka
Dashuri	Homo
საყვარელი	inimene
אהבה	ihminen
Amo	l'humain
Amour	ადამიანი
Habibi	Kanaka
maitasun	Duine
rakkaus	मानव
愛	Humano
любовь	l'umano
Սեր	människan
Liewe	человек
miłość	con người
Aşk	људски
Liebe	τον άνθρωπο
Love	Mënsch

La vita è piena di cose positive e negative. E che ti piaccia o no, avrà sempre i suoi alti e bassi. A volte sembrerà che la sfortuna ti stia inseguendo in profondità. Come se il mondo fosse coperto da un velo grigio e la luce del sole fosse infinitamente lontana. Ma anche quello andrà via. Credimi. Non è per niente che la gente dice che la vita è troppo breve. Perché ciò che conta alla fine è come hai affrontato questi eventi negativi. Non mollare mai, vivere, trarre il meglio da tutto, rimanere forte, amare e imparare a lasciarsi andare, aggrapparsi alle cose buone e cercare di essere felice. Anche se ti sembra di non poter mai essere più felice. Ma tu puoi.

Life is too short
To be wasted.
Life is
And can
Be beautiful.
As long as you make the right thing of it.
- Hakuna Matata

The breeze of warm
Relaxing wind.

Sounds of the ocean.
Waves smoothly touching the sand.

Olfaction of spring's flowers.
Colors of born nature.

Intensity of a cloudless sun.
The sky covered in deep blue.

Looking upon the horizon,
Birds filling marrows with music.

Heaven rising up underneath your feet.

...Festivals
Deep conversations
Laughing so much that your belly hurts
Going to the movies
Listening to Music
Soul
RnB
Rock
Jazz
Pop
Trap
Dancing around like crazy
Singing in the shower
First bite when you're hungry
Family
Friends
Exploring new places
Adrenaline
Rollercoaster
Getting out of the plane
Coffee time
Going to work
Spontaneous adventures
Sounds of Rain
Animals
First snow
Success
Forehead kisses
Naked feet on Grass
Divorcing
Learning new things
After a long day going to Sleep
Children's laughter
Cities
Warm and tight hugs
Being around people you love
Time to yourself
Concerts
Cooking
Making others happy
Sex
Driving around without having any plan
Cozy Nights
Amusement parks
Time
Random Compliments
Marrying
Seeing somebody again after a long time
Moving
Nature
Spreading love
Doing good without expecting anything back...

Where the ocean meets the sky
I'll find you my love.
One Day,
We will reach the width
And form one.

Tell them you love them
Before
One day
It's too late
To do so.

111314
I want to say
Thank you
For always loving me
No matter what.
I want to say
Thank you
For always pulling me up again,
While I ceased to exist.
I want to say
thank you
Thank you
For everything
Cause without you
I couldn't imagine living
- Remember that I will always love you

05
I know I never showed you my love
Made you feel like I hated you
Hating you for existing.
I'm sorry for never telling you
That I wouldn't change you for a thing.
That I love you.
Loving you more than anything.

Between all this
Misery and
All these
False people
You could
Oversee
The ones
Who are there
On your good
As well as
Bad days.
You could
Oversee
A gaiety
That has been there
The whole time.
- look more closely

I've been through a lot in my life.
And most of these moments,
Where it felt like
I was trapped in a darkness
That was literally smothering me,
You have been there.

There is a particular amount
Of people
And things
That can be like lightning on your murkiest days.

I don't need
Millions of Dollars,
Hundreds of friends,
Numerous presents,
You are more than enough.

- _____ , thank you.

So, if you reached the end of this.
Where most of the stuff just felt fucked up.
Then let me tell you one thing:
Fuck what other say
And just love yourself,
Appreciate the things you have
And the ones who value you,
The same way you admire them.
Because life is way too precious
To give a damn about all these negative things.
Now baby,
Start seeing the colors.

Accept.
Understand.
Respect.
Be good.
Strong.
Self-confident.
Tolerant.
Beautiful.
Kind.
Special.
Maybe even ambitious.
Free.
Loyal.
And most importantly
Love.

Life is compendiously,
Mortal,
Instant,
Even esoteric.
It can be hard.
Yes,
But also fucking amazing.

So, it's okay